DO OR DO NOT

HOW TO IMPROVISE LIKE A JEDI

BY MARY CARPENTER

Do Or Do Not

How to Improvise Like a Jedi

Copyright © Mary Carpenter

All rights reserved.
No part of this book may be reproduced or used in any manner without written permission of the copyright owner except for use of quotations in a book review.

First paperback edition March 2019

Cover Design by Kristin Finger

ISBN 978-1-7336323-0-0

For More information and to purchase go to:

maryccarpenter.com

Contents

Acknowledgments	i
Introduction	iii
"A Long Time Ago in a Galaxy Far Far Away"	1
"You know that little droid is going to cause me a lot of trouble"	6
"Aren't you a little short for a stormtrooper?"	12
"Stay on target."	14
"Stretch out with your feelings"	20
"Into the garbage chute flyboy."	23
"You're all clear kid, now let's blow this thing and go home."	29
"Do or do not, there is no try."	33
"So certain are you. Always with you it cannot be done."	35
"That's no moon, it's a space station."	40
"Who is the more foolish, the fool or the fool who follows him"	45
"Never tell me the odds."	49
"The more you tighten your grip, the more star systems will slip through your fingers"	53
"There are alternatives to fighting."	56
"All his life has he looked away…to the future, to the horizon. Never his mind on where he was…Hmmm? On what he was doing."	58
"Watch your mouth kid or you'll find yourself floating home."	61
"Laugh it up, Fuzzball"	62
"I don't know who you are or where you came from, but from now on, you do as I tell you."	63

"Great Kid! Don't get cocky."   66

"But with the blast shield down I can't see, how am I supposed to
    fight?"   70

"We're doomed."   74

"The Force is what gives a Jedi his power. It's an energy field created by
    all living things. It surrounds us and penetrates us. It binds the galaxy
    together."   78

"The Force will be with you, always."   81

Quotations   82

Acknowledgements

We all know that improv is a team sport, and so too is this book. Collaboration makes everything better, and I am so very grateful to Jill Bernard, Ann Jackman, Richard Jackman, Micheline McManus, Megan Bellwoar-Hollinger, Karen Getz, Rob Morris, Rachel Miller and Jim Carpenter for there valuable feedback. Boundless gratitude to Alli Soowal for her editing and proofreading prowess. An enormous thank you to Kristin Finger for her graphic design. I must also recognize CSZ Philadelphia for being my creative home since 1992; they have made me a better storyteller, teacher, and human being. And to Mike Young, thank you for being my Obi Wan Kenobi.

"An elegant weapon for a more civilized age"

-Obi Wan Kenobi

The first time I saw a lightsaber on screen was awesome. It was elegant, mesmerizing, dangerous and cool. It wasn't a grand ceremonious reveal either, Obi Wan simply pulled it out of an old trunk in his humble hut on Tatooine. And in an instant, a door to the past was opened and the future glimpsed all at once linked by the blue glow of this elegant weapon. Context and curiosity with the simple push of a button.

The first time I tried improv was awesome. It was energizing, mesmerizing, dangerous and cool. It wasn't a grand ceremonious reveal, it was just an exercise in a sophomore acting class at Northwestern. In an instant I felt completely comfortable and totally naive all at once; and I was hooked. Context and curiosity with the simple introduction of Freeze Tag.

It is fair to say that most of my life has been guided by *Star Wars* and Improv. The crossover was inevitable, if unexpected. It happened unceremoniously again. I was simply teaching a class and found myself
clarifying a point by saying "The more you tighten your grip, the more star systems will slip through your fingers." It was the clearest way to illustrate the futility of control. And then the floodgate was open. *Star Wars* found its way into my teaching time and time again.

Hence the book.

You do not need to be a *Star Wars* fan to understand this book. Each chapter starts with a quote from one of the movies. All of the quotes are from the original trilogy, Episodes IV-VI, and they inspire the discoveries in each chapter; much like a suggestion from the audience inspires your improv, much like the lightsaber piqued Luke's interest. You can still understand this book if you haven't seen the movies.

First and foremost, this is a book about improv. I love improv; the simplicity, the clarity, the impossibility. The infinity of it has shaped my career, my creativity, and, let's just go for it folks, my life. It promises the potential of everything asking in return only that we take all that we know and all that we are and jump into the unknown. Into a galaxy far far away.

So "Punch it Chewy."

"A Long Time Ago in a Galaxy Far Far Away"

Opening scroll, Platform, Who-What-Where-Why, Context, no matter what you call it, you've got to have it. At the top of a scene you need to know what the status quo is, what is the normal in this world. The more specific the better. We need to know that "It is a period of civil war" and that "During the battle, Rebel spies managed to steal secret plans to the Empire's ultimate weapon, the DEATH STAR" and that "Princess Leia races home aboard her starship, custodian of the stolen plans that can save her people and restore freedom to the galaxy" Those specifics instantly orient us to the world of *Star Wars*. They give us a structure and context and still leave tons of room for discovery, complications and surprises.

So how do you begin improvising? Begin by giving some context. Often we flounder at the top of a scene either hesitant to declare information because we do not trust our instincts or believe our idea is good enough, or we wallow in the realm of the "organic evolution."

I'm going to let you in on a secret right now: your idea is good enough. We (meaning your fellow improvisers and the audience) currently have no information whatsoever, so whatever you say or do will not be wrong. In fact, the more specific you are, the more grateful we are because now we have something to go on. And as for organic evolution, I'm all for patience and allowing the answers to present themselves, but if you're really listening and paying attention those answers are presenting themselves from the moment you get the suggestion from the audience, from the second you make eye contact with the other person or people on stage. You have a reaction, you form an impression, you know who that person is in relation to you, you know where you are and why you're there. So reveal that discovery you've made in that instant. Organic does not mean interminably slow, it just means being honest and present and naming what exists in that moment. So, getting back to how you begin any improv, short form, long form, Terraform, if you're initiating, define something specific about this new world you are discovering for the first time.

- Give your partner a name. It can even be their name, or you can give them a title like: grandma, or Boss, or Rabbi. By endowing them, you are giving them the gift of helping them discover who they are.

- Engage in the environment with an actual activity apart from standing around and talking. If you're in a kitchen, make a salad or load the dishwasher or unload the groceries. If you're on the space station, calibrate the machines or plot a course or unload the groceries. By defining your space and engaging in an activity, you create action that demands reaction.
- Declare the emotional reaction you just had to your partner walking on stage. When your fellow improviser enters, are you glad? Sad? Mad? Scared? Confused? State that fact, it instantly gives your partner something to respond to.
- Make a clear non-verbal offer that communicates point of view, location or activity. You do not have to speak to communicate elements of the platform. Shrug your shoulders while you pack your suitcase, it connects you to your partner immediately because it implies point of view.
- Make a strong character choice that opens the door to time, relationship, location or point of view. Be Sherlock Holmes, or the judgmental aunt, or the pilot on Air Force One. The specificity will help orient your partner(s).

You don't have to get the whole scroll out, in fact it's often more fun if you don't. You might just get out "A long time ago in a galaxy far far away." That's fine, that's plenty, because now you have engaged your partner's imagination. They are already filling in some blanks. With your one definition, this new world has come into sharper focus for them, and they can define another part of it.

So what's your responsibility if you are receiving the first offer? Accept it, of course, duh. And then the next step is to build on, to "and" it. You now have to choose a side:
- One filled with fear of making a mistake or treading on what you perceive to be your partner's obviously well planned out idea. What if you define something they did not intend? Surely disaster will befall you both.
- Or one that is still a bit fuzzy, but your instinct is revealing another specific about this new world unfolding in front of you.

Which side do you choose? Well, young Padawan, we all know that "Fear is the path to the dark side. Fear leads to anger. Anger leads to hate. Hate leads to suffering." And who needs suffering? Do not fear treading on a path that is only partially laid out. If your partner had all the answers, they would have spelled them out. They threw out one, maybe two pieces of information. You got intrigued, you saw something more based on their initial idea, so trust it, add to it, and run with it. Your partner will be grateful because they really only had the one idea. Now you both have many ideas, and before you know it, droids are being jettisoned in escape pods and there is no turning back.

Whether you've only seen one Star Wars movie, or all of them, the anticipation of that opening scroll is delicious and exciting. We can't wait to gather the information that will form the basis for this prequel or sequel. Context is a miraculous thing. It does not limit our possibilities, it defines the realm of the playground in which we get to play, and it is always punctuated with an adventurous ...

> **"You know that little droid is going to cause me a lot of trouble."**
> *-Luke Skywalker*

Gee, I hope so.

That one line is a promise to the audience. It is a promise that we are going to see some trouble. And that's what we paid for. Star Wars would not have been nearly as interesting if Luke fixed the droids and they worked out perfectly on the farm and everyone shared a good laugh as they sat down to a nice meal of blended cabbage and blue milk.

We want trouble when we go to movies or plays or improv shows. We crave it, and even though we want things to turn out well for everyone, we don't want to see that right away. We want them to get into a mess for awhile and see how they handle it.

So why is it that so many improvisers spend an inordinate amount of time talking about trouble, talking about action, talking about "what we're gonna do," and never doing it? We, as humans, spend every day over-thinking every move we make, every word we say, every action we might take. When we go to see a movie or play or improv show, we want to see people actually doing the things we think about doing, saying the things we long to say, making the move we're dying to make. We want to see the mess and the struggle and the potential triumph or disaster. We want to recognize ourselves and either commiserate or be inspired.

So, young and old Jedis alike, do something. How? Here we go.

The basics:
- Start with context (opening scroll). Be confident in whatever normal you set up.
- Discover trouble (stolen plans to Death Star). Trouble is anything that upsets the status quo or "normal" you have established.
- In an attempt to authentically solve the trouble, everything you do makes it worse. This is called heightening; ie: looking for the sand people, jumping into the garbage chute, blasting the controls that extend the bridge, etc. Heightening causes deeper trouble and more heightening leads to a climax of

>   realization, which recognizes or necessitates change (destroying the Death Star).
> - As the dust settles a "new normal" is revealed (closing tableau, Luke gets to wear big boy pants)

There is your basic structure for any play, movie, epic literary classic and improv scene.

The key to all of this is to recognize and heighten the trouble. (By the way, I say trouble instead of conflict because conflict implies argument and not all trouble has to be an argument.) The best way to recognize or discover trouble is to be in the location you define, having the relationship you establish and doing an activity; when something happens to make the little voice inside you say "huh…?! That was interesting or different or fascinating!" That is your trouble. And now you must name it, commit to it, wallow in it.

The trouble with trouble is believing that it is trouble enough.

Often, in an attempt to be interesting and gain the audience's favor, we invent trouble. We panic, afraid nothing is happening and that we're being boring, so we invent a broken leg or a dragon or aliens from outer space, which rarely make sense given the context you so painstakingly set up. Trouble can start with someone looking at you differently, or saying something with an unexpected tone (doesn't have to be negative). Trouble does not necessarily have to be:

- bodily injury
- an alien invasion
- a police chase
- losing a contact lens

It *can* be any of those things, but it can also be as subtle as an unexpected act of kindness, or falling in love with the wrong person, or becoming jealous about your sibling becoming your parents' favorite, etc. It is the unexpected wrinkle that made your eyes widen a little more and caused you to take a breath of surprise.

Once identified, you need to be invested in this trouble. You need to want things to succeed. Something has to be at stake. You need to pursue its evolution or resolution with relentless fervor as only your character would. You don't need to take time out to comment on it or trivialize it with cleverness. You need to try and solve, resolve and/or explore it in a genuine desire to seek an outcome, and yet everything you do heightens its complications. Throughout this pursuit your efforts reveal your character's flaws, strengths, and all the unique parts that make him or her human, while we as audience members ooh and ahh and recognize ourselves and our flaws and fabulousness.

Okay, let's break it down:

- Context: Luke, Han & Chewie, disguised as stormtroopers (Chewie as their prisoner), go to Detention Block AA23 to rescue Princess Leia. What is at stake? Their lives.
- Trouble: The guards there do not have any record of a prisoner transfer and go to check. Han, Luke and Chewie start shooting.
- Ways they heighten
    o Han tries to lie his way through a conversation over the intercom
    o Han shoots the intercom
    o Real stormtroopers arrive
    o Everyone gets trapped in the corridor
    o Leia shoots a hole in the wall
    o They all jump in the garbage chute which leads to…
- More trouble. A new normal that they then heighten again in their genuine desire to escape.

Luke, Han & Chewie were not trying to get into trouble. On the contrary, they were trying to rescue the princess without incident. Everything they did was an attempt to save the Princess and not get caught. And it was fun and exciting because it made sense.

Here's a simple scientific-looking but in fact not scientifically proven formula:

- Trouble + Investment + Action + Reaction = More Action = Fun

We're not done yet. There are the Lukes & Hans, the ones dealing first hand with the trouble; and then there are the heighteners: the detention block supervisor, the stormtroopers, etc. If you are the improvisers on the back line or offstage, what is your job? Help facilitate trouble if necessary, and once it has been discovered, help to heighten it. Nine times out of ten, the main characters will discover trouble on their own; if they don't, you have a wider lens off stage to help reveal trouble based on the context set up. However, when trouble is uncovered, your job is now to help heighten it. Be patient; don't intrude. You must allow time for each new complication to take hold and resonate and lead to the next complication based on the new context. It's not dog pile on the rabbit time. The best guide is to simply ask yourself "what does the story need next?"

Trouble is good in improv. It is fun. It makes the story happen. Be patient, pay attention, allow trouble to be revealed, and when you feel yourself go "huh?!....." jump into the garbage chute flyboy.

"Aren't you a little short for a stormtrooper?"
-Princess Leia

So, says Princess Leia when she first sees Luke. No you're not too short. And you're not too old to be an ingenue. You're not too tall to be a three year old. You're not too human to be a bear. You're not too manly to be a girl. And you're not too girly to be a man. In improv you can play any character, even yourself.

I'm terrible at playing characters. I would have been spotted as a fake stormtrooper immediately. I never stop trying though, and I never limit myself. In addition to the standards (moms, girlfriends, store clerks, neighbors, kids), I've been whales, Igors, garden gnomes, jerks, ghosts, deranged birds. And boy was it fun.

It is easy to get locked into playing the same things over and over again, or to limit yourself because of how you look or want to be seen by the audience. The sooner you can let that go, the better.

You must do what the scene, game or moment requires. Which means that you have to relish the risk of being unlikeable, or looking like an idiot, or looking unattractive, or going from a British accent to a southern accent mid-character because you can't do accents (no I'm not talking about me, just a really good friend of mine who looks a lot like me). The sooner you can shed the need to be liked by the audience, the freer and more playful your improv will be.

So, go for it, just commit. Grab a point of view, commit, get your body involved, commit, try an accent, commit, commit, commit. You're 5 foot 2 inches? Why not play Shaquille O'Neal? Shy girl-next-door? Of course you can pull off Gene Simmons from Kiss. Slightly overweight middle aged woman? You bet you can play a teenage heartthrob. Scrawny farm boy from Tatooine? Hell yeah you can pass for a stormtrooper and save your sister who you don't know is your sister, so you kind of have an inappropriate crush on her. If Luke hadn't even tried, that's a can of worms we never would have enjoyed.

> **"Stay on target."**
>
> *-Garven Dreis*

The rebel fighters had a very specific goal at the end of *Star Wars: Episode IV A New Hope*: destroy the Death Star by shooting a proton torpedo through an exhaust port roughly two meters wide. That was their objective.

Objectives are important in improv. Characters need to want something, because what you want determines what you do, and how you do what you do to get what you want determines who you are. For example:

- Luke Skywalker and Red Leader Garven Dreis (had to look up that name, I'm not that much of a *Star Wars* geek) both wanted to shoot their photon torpedos into the exhaust port successfully.

- Here's how Garven did it
  - He went into the trench with his two wingmen, Red 10 & Red 12. They tried to hold off Vader and his TIE fighters while Dreis switched on his targeting computer. Red 10 & Red 12 fought valiantly, but were shot down. Dreis remained focused, followed procedure, gave updates ("Almost there….almost there") and got a shot off. He pulled out of the trench only to see that he just missed the target. He was then shot from the sky and his Fighter disintegrated in a fiery explosion on the surface of the Death Star.
- Here's what we can assume about Garven's character based on how he went after his objective:
  - He is a good soldier
  - He is calm under pressure which leads us to believe that he is experienced
  - He follows procedure
  - He is focused
  - He perseveres even when his wingmen go down
  - He never gives up
- Here's how Luke did it:

- Since the rest of the Red Squadron had been killed and it was just down to Luke, Wedge Antilles and Biggs Darklighter, Luke did not hesitate to take the lead. He gave clear instructions on an impromptu plan and kept his wingmen focused and encouraged. Once they entered the trench, Luke turned on his targeting computer and began his run for the exhaust port. Biggs was shot down and Wedge's ship was damaged leaving Luke on his own. He is all alone, completely responsible, and at a loss, until he hears Obi Wan's voice. Following the great Jedi's guidance, Luke shuts off his targeting computer and trusts the Force to guide him. With a little help from Han Solo, Luke takes his shot and destroys the Death Star

  - Here's what we can assume about Luke's character based on how he went after his objective:
    - He thinks and acts impulsively
    - He has natural leadership qualities
    - He is brave
    - He is determined He is selfless
    - He trusts his instincts

- He never gives up
- He is unconventional

Both characters had the same goal, but how they went about achieving that goal distinguished their characters.

Characters on stage must want something, otherwise why are we watching them? Nobody wants to make the effort to put pants on and go out to watch people kind of wanting something, but it's ok if they don't get it because their casual nature will seem contradictory and therefore funny. Yawn! It is so much more satisfying to see characters on stage really want something and go after it with full passion and human fallibility.

As improvisers we often spend a good deal of our time on stage focusing on narrative; a sense of story and structure and what is needed is vital. What drives story, all story, is strong characters who want something and the actions they employ to get what they want. Stories are made of people wanting/needing something desperately, going for it, falling down, learning from their fall and trying again. Princess Leia wants to stop the Empire, so she steals the plans to the Death Star, and when her ship is boarded she hides them in R2D2 and sends him down to Tatooine. Story is driven by character. Characters' objectives and actions create circumstances that drive stories to the next level, i.e., a farm boy on Tatooine finds a droid and winds up saving the galaxy. Bottom line, your character in any improv scene or game must want something, and that something must be important to them. How they go about getting what they want reveals character. As an improviser, you are constantly discovering your character as you create them. A great way to discover who they are is by deciding what they want and why they want it. Your character's investment in what they want will determine their tactics and their emotional life. So basically:

- Strong objective leads to tactics
- Tactics lead to success or failure
- Success or failure leads to emotional reaction
- Emotional reaction leads to new tactics and sometimes the discovery of a new objective

This can work in any scene or game. Whether it is short form or long form, gimmick game or scene based, having an objective helps ground your work and bring it to life.

- Playing Spelling Bee? What happens to the energy of the game if your spelling bee champion really wants to do well to prove to everyone they deserve to be champion? What if they are trying to impress someone in the audience? Suddenly the game changes from a general gimmick to an engaging character study.
- Stuck in a scene that is going nowhere? Ask yourself in that moment, what does my character want to do right now? Kick over a table in frustration? Steal all the cookies and eat them before anyone notices? Make this person fall in love with me? Whatever the answer is, grab onto it and run with it. The scene wakes up and you have a clear path

- Watching on the sidelines and trying to figure out what the scene needs? Ask yourself what the main characters want. Once you answer that, moving the narrative along becomes easier. How can you thwart their goals? How can you place obstacles/trouble for them to overcome? How can you help them achieve their goals?

A character is not just a combination of random quirks and traits. Quirks and traits are a great place to start, but, I promise, if you throw in a strong objective, those quirks and traits will find greater specificity, quirkiness and fun than if you just keep repeating the same bit over and over. Have an objective. Want something with everything you've got. Stay on target, and see if you can save the galaxy.

"Stretch out with your feelings"
-Obi Wan Kenobi

So says the wise old Jedi.

But feelings aren't funny. They aren't clever. They aren't hip. They don't go with my torn jeans and carefully chosen to not look carefully chosen t-shirt.

Maybe. But feelings are universally identifiable. We've all had them. We've all expressed them to varying levels of success and awkwardness. And, ladies and gentlemen, I promise you they will raise the stakes in any improv scene you do. Some of the best improv instruction I ever received, thanks to Mr. Joe Bill, was "The quickest way out of your head is to go into your heart."

It makes brilliant and beautiful sense. Thinking is all about ourselves and figuring out something in a very singular fashion that makes sense to us. But to feel necessarily means to feel something about someone or something. It takes our focus outward. Yes it makes us vulnerable and exposed, but emotion is action, it is movement forward in some direction. It is not an intellectual pursuit. It is not two people standing around talking and proving how clever they are. Because, between you and me and the rest of the universe, an audience kind of hates it when folks on stage are working inexhaustibly hard to prove how much smarter they are than the paying audience. But to see someone dare to feel something hugely or awkwardly or unsuccessfully or even successfully, we can all connect to that. We spend our lives talking around things and delaying action for fear of repercussion. We want desperately to express our undying love to that co-worker or old college friend, or neighbor's spouse, but we rarely act on it. But to see someone do that on stage, well that's fun to watch. That brings me forward in my seat. That makes me want more.

So hard to do it as an improviser though, especially when the other improviser may just make a clever joke out of it. Yes, you may get your heart broken, but better to have loved and lost, right. So, the next time you feel the scene stagnate express the emotion your character feels:

- Declare your love
- Name your fear
- State your confusion
- Vent your frustration

And don't stop there. Ride the wave of what you're feeling and allow your partner's response to heighten that feeling accordingly. It's impossible not to have some kind of emotional response to an emotional declaration in real life and on stage. The stakes are instantly raised when you do this and the sediment of the stagnated moment of your scene has been shifted. Action is generally more interesting than discussion and emotion requires action because everyone has a reaction to emotion.

If you want to be a better improviser you must be willing to risk everything; looking like a fool, failing, not being the audience's favorite. And you must risk your heart. So stretch out with your feelings Luke; even with the blast shield down you will know what to do.

"Into the garbage chute flyboy."

-Princess Leia

I have a confession to make. One of the things I hate most about many improv shows I see is that they happen in some nebulous undefined place where the only activity seems to be talking to each other about why we can't do this or that. What bugs me about it?

- Improvisers not engaging in their environment
- Improvisers stalling action

Both of the above lead to something many improvisers complain about: being in their head. They also lead to boring scene-work and bad habits and a perpetuation of clever over honest. So let's get into this.

Engaging in Your Environment

In real life when we have a conversation with someone, we are in a specific location. We are also usually doing something in that location. Even if we are standing at a bar, we are in a place and we have a response to that place. Environment matters in improv. It is another character in the scene and your relationship to and interaction with that environment can literally change the course of any scene and unlock parts of your imagination without you even trying.

You do not have to be an accomplished mime or physical comedian to bring an environment to life on an improv stage. You simply need to see where you are, what is there and why it is relevant to the scene or game that is going on in the moment. You don't have to invent anything; instead, practice discovery, just practice seeing things.

How do you create environment on a blank improv stage with minimal mime training? Simple, keep in mind two things: environment is defined by what is in that space, and how you use and relate to the objects in that space. We have relationships to spaces both familiar and unfamiliar and that affects how we relate to the people in those spaces and what happens between you and those people. When you walk into your own kitchen you know where things are, how everything operates, how to load the dishwasher, etc; when you walk into your girlfriend or boyfriend's parents' kitchen for the first time, you have a much different response and investment. Already the stakes are higher. You can create that same tension with nothing but a chair or a couple of stools on a blank stage by how you sit and what you see around you. Once again think about discovery vs. invention. See what is on the coffee table in front of you. Yes I know it's not actually there. So try this right now.

- Find a relatively open neutral-ish space to work
- Wherever you are sitting close your eyes
- When you open your eyes you are in your best friend's grandmother's house for the first time. You are in the living room.
- Where is the couch? What color is it? What kind of shape is it in, new old, worn, etc.?
- Where is the coffee table? What is on it?
- Pick something up from the coffee table. If it can open, open it up. What's inside?
- What other furniture is in the room?
- Are there any pictures? If so, walk over and look at them. Which one do you want to ask the grandmother about?
- And so on...

You can do this exercise with any environment you choose: a miniature golf course, a classroom, the Oval Office. Practice looking outward and seeing rather than struggling to invent. Once you can see the environment, you can engage with it. What new information can you discover to move the scene, relationship, story forward?

Stalling Action

How often have you been in a scene and found yourself negotiating your next step? Playing the "what if" or the "but wait" game. You talk around doing something. I don't know if people stall action to be funny, or because they want to make complete sense of it before they do it or because they fear messing it up. Secret time: you're supposed to mess it up, something's supposed to go wrong, so there's no reason to avoid doing it.

Star Wars would have sucked if Luke and Obi Wan had just stayed in their hut talking about destroying the Empire. There's not a lot of standing around and talking/negotiating in Star Wars. From the get go folks are busy defending ships, hiding behind walls, traversing Tatooine's arid desert, and so on. They are not just sitting around talking about what to do next, they are doing it; which is why we keep watching it over and over again.

Luke, Leia, Han and Chewie don't stand around talking about their next move when they seem destined to be captured by the stormtroopers as they huddle in the corridor of the detention block. Instead plucky self-sufficient Leia sees the tools in front of her - a blaster - and alters the environment by blowing a hole in the wall, and into the garbage chute they all go. This action leads to the next bit of "what the what" as the environment of the garbage chute complicates their adventure further. They mix who they are with where they are and what they want in order to discover their next move.

Simple right?

Not always.

For most improvisers the element of the context they most often neglect is the environment. They simply stand around discussing their relationship in some void. Sometimes they do identify their environment and stand around looking at it talking about what they should do. They fear specificity and action. So, often, we find ourselves in scenes where we talk about where we are and talk about what we should do, yet never actually do it. And we're back to inventing what the scene is about, which is exhausting and usually not fun for performers or the audience. Next time you find yourself doing that, try discovering what's right in front of you, try doing that thing someone suggested to do, and see what it leads to.

Discovery vs. Invention. The best way to discover is to look outward. Be in a place doing something specific with someone specific and see what happens. How would:

- Two people who are attracted to each other make a sandwich together?
- Two colleagues up for the same promotion search for a lost file?
- A legendary Jedi disable a tractor beam with two stormtroopers standing guard?

Take your hands out of your pockets and dig into the space around you. Do not fear what your action will lead to, be excited about what you have yet to discover. Stalling action isn't fun or clever. It is a form of coitus interruptus. You've made a promise to the audience by introducing the prospect of something happening, don't back away. The classic example is when an improviser produces a gun in a scene. If you're going to do that you better be prepared to use it rather than taking the safe and lame way out by saying "No wait…" Okay I'll wait, but this better be better than what you promised me when you showed me that gun? And it never is better.

Be somewhere, have a response to that somewhere, and do something. Jump into the garbage chute and explore it like Magellan. It will reveal wonders, like a cycloptic, periscopic water monster, if you engage with it.

"You're all clear kid, now let's blow this thing and go home."
-Han Solo

This is the part of *Star Wars: Episode IV A New Hope* when I fell in love with Han Solo. I liked him from the start, don't get me wrong; irreverent scoundrel with a sense of humor...yes please. But it was that hopeless moment when Darth Vader had Luke in his sights and then Han shows up out of nowhere and makes Luke's triumph possible.

Support. Many improvisers fear this word because they think it is synonymous with the words 'boring' or 'unmemorable.' Ahhhh, but support is what it's all about. When you can get out of your way enough to fully support and lift up another player's offer, character or game, when you are more invested in the successful completion of the mission to destroy the Death Star instead of simply paying off your debts to Jabba the Hutt, well my friends, that is when you have arrived and will most likely go on to star in the Indiana Jones and Jack Ryan franchises.

I was rehearsing an improv show once and I was just so stuck. Ironically, I was the most experienced improviser in the cast, but I just felt so unfunny and that I was letting everyone else down. Then it hit me, I didn't have to be funny because everyone around me was already hilarious. I just needed to support them, and the show would be great. Guess what happened when I tried that, my offers and actions became more interesting, surprising, and, yes, funny.

- Instead of trying to be fascinating I became fascinated by everyone else and the story evolving in front of me. I focused on what was happening outside my head.
- Instead of worrying about my own performance, I made it my goal to make everyone else look great, I made the scene about the other person. I supported and heightened their offers.
- Instead of trying to be original, I focused on being honest and obvious.

As a result, improv became so much more fun, and the improv universe was suddenly huge and limitless.

This is when I really fell in love with improv. Oh I loved it before, but on a much more superficial level. Here is why I fell deeply in love. Whether you're alone on stage and supporting your own offers and the energy from the audience, or you are surrounded by an ensemble of unique and flawed and fabulous improvisers, it is the moment to moment support, celebration and expansion of each other's offers that creates this once in a lifetime moment that can never be recreated. That moment that we all hope for, when a genuine connection has been made, and it yields a collective awe at the recognition or surprise generated from a band of players fiercely exploring something bigger than themselves.

To support is to be completely open and present to the human being in front of you. To dare to make a connection and be more interested in them than you are in yourself. It doesn't mean you can't disagree or seek clarity or be confused because in that moment, supporting their offer might necessitate you being the bad guy or the one who thwarts their hopes and dreams because that is what the story requires. Support means to relish that morsel of an idea in front of you, even if it's just a shrug or someone moving a chair or a one-word offer, and add yourself to it so that together you can see where it leads. You do not have to try to be interesting, because everything you are is interesting enough. Your response will automatically be unique because there is no one else quite like you. Your support of the offer at hand will look different than Cool Woman with multiple piercings who always knows exactly what to say, and Whip Smart Sarcastic Guy whose every word is hilarious, because you are all your own you's and you are all fascinating.

So the next time you are in that moment and in your head and asking yourself, what would be interesting or what would be funny, just blast Darth Vader out of the way and focus on the person in front of you. Help Luke destroy the Death Star. Jabba can wait.

"Do or do not, there is no try."

-Yoda

Yoda... who knew he was an improv master too?

That is right, Do. Please for the sake of the audience and your fellow improvisers, Do something, anything.

To try is to negotiate and doubt. "I'll try it," asserts an implicit disclaimer that you are not responsible for whatever happens next. Yes there is also a kind of courage in trying something new, absolutely, bravo. But trying is only partial commitment, and improv simply will not work with partial commitment. Trying implies that you have already accepted failure, that you have already given in, that you do not believe in the Force.

Doing, however, is active. It is an action. And action leads to reaction which leads to more action, and suddenly our X-Wing is out of the swamps and we can go save Han and Leia. Doing in the face of fear is bravery even if the result is disastrous and you get frozen in carbonite. Trying is safe, it is acceptable, and it is controllable. Many good improv shows are full of trying. Trying sets acceptable limits. Doing dares to bust those limits apart until we bump into new ones and figure out how to break those down too. Doing dreams of the possible. Trying accepts the impossible. Remember:

    Luke: You ask for the impossible. I don't believe it.

    Yoda: That is why you fail.

> **"So certain are you. Always with you it cannot be done."**
>
> *-Yoda*

Listening is a vital skill for every improviser. How, who and what we choose to listen to expands or shrinks our improv world accordingly.

We all think we are good listeners, and, for the everyday nuts and bolts, we probably are. Improv, however, requires 360° surround sound listening and awareness. 3D-ing these skills takes a little intention and practice; you not only have to listen acutely to the improvisers with whom you are playing, you must also, just as importantly, learn to listen to yourself.

Listening to your fellow players immerses you in the context of the game, scene, story, world. Listening acutely with ears, mind, eyes, body and soul allows the realm of what's possible to become clear. When I say listen acutely I do not mean to tense up and furrow your brow and bear down. Listening acutely works better if you can let go, breathe and simply fall in love and be fascinated with everything that is done and said right in front of you. Even if you are confused, you can still be fascinated.

In order to do this, you must silence your judges' table. This is the panel of you seated in your brain that shouts loudly about why this idea or that idea won't work. It is the panel of whiners who ask "why isn't my partner taking the scene where I wanted it to go?" It is the bickering throng who sing in cacophonous chorus "It cannot be done." Your judge's table may initially sound like voices of reason, but they are actually control freaks ruled by fear of the unknown. You must not be swayed by them. Turn off their microphones and leave their conference room.

Once you've left, focus on your partners and truly listen.

To truly listen is to take in information; we are all capable of this and we do it in our own individual ways. Some of us gather, process and store information mathematically; some of us are big picture thinkers; some of us synthesize information through empathy; and so on, and so on, and so on. You know how you think, you were probably told or given clues constantly in school. So first identify how you take in information.

Next, don't worry about it. It's useful to know so that you can have confidence in the ideas that come your way. It might also be interesting to you as you grow as an improviser to either expand how you listen, or learn how fellow improvisers listen. The reason you don't have to worry about it or try hard to do it is because you've been doing it your whole life. The best way to listen in improv is to be less interested in yourself and more interested in what's happening in front of you.

Now onto the harder task, listening to yourself. Not your judge's table, but your instinct. The key to improv is to identify, trust and act on your instinct in an instant. In order to identify that instinct you must listen to that little voice in your head that says "I think *this* is true." The *"this"* is the idea that is inspired by the fascination in the scene, game, story, moment, etc., which is gleaned from listening to your partner(s). It may be logical or illogical, that will be determined by the perspective of those watching. But in your experience that *"this"* is what feels true for this moment. When you hear that voice, which speaks very quickly, the hardest job you have as an improviser is before you; you must *trust* that voice. You must believe in its value and its potential for expanding the breadth of the possible without questioning its originality. You must believe you can raise your X-Wing from the swamps with the Force.

Luke: I don't believe it.

Yoda: That is why you fail.

Once you believe in your idea you must add it to the mix and remain open to how it is incorporated and open yourself up to the next idea.

All of this happens impossibly fast. Most of the time you respond without thinking, you trust without knowing. And then every now and then that idea pops into your head and you fear it seems too crazy or weird or outside your basic everyday operating system. That idea popped in there because you are becoming more flexible, because by being fascinated instead of trying to be fascinating your world is a little bit bigger. You have created space for new discoveries. And these discoveries are like toys on your birthday. So play with them.

And now for the third D in the 3-D listening equation. You must learn to listen in and to silence. Listening does not just happen with our ears. As mentioned earlier, we also listen and take in information with our eyes, with our body, with our mind. The insight that can be accumulated during silence is staggering. As improvisers, we are often afraid of silence, for many of the same reasons we fear it in life.

- It feels awkward
- We're afraid we are not being understood
- It feels vulnerable

It can be awkward, you might be misunderstood and it demands vulnerability, but the communication that happens in silence is often crystal clear and always richer and more riveting than all the words we use. We have all been in that situation in life when we are searching for the right words and there are none. We have also been in the situation when no words are needed and yet everything is understood.

In rehearsal, practice or class try doing a series of silent scenes. These are not scenes where the volume is turned down and you are mouthing words, these are scenes in which you are not allowed to use words. Sound is okay, as long as you are not using sounds as a gibberish-like crutch, but they are results of reactions or emotions. These scenes require great patience. All the foundation of scene work is the same as in talking scenes; you must make assumptions as to who you are, what you are doing and what you want from the other person. You must work slowly at first until you master this new language. I am not talking about clowning or mime. Those skills are incredible and can help in silent scenes, but I am talking about building relationship, investment and heightening without words. It is hard, and it is immensely satisfying. Try it. Fail at it. Try it many more times. It will deepen your ability to listen on all levels.

Once you start really listening with all of your senses and being fascinated and loving the ideas you discover, they don't seem illogical to you or your judges' table, they seem like they were supposed to happen. And since everyone's illogical is unique to them, you wind up with a pretty spectacular one of a kind collection of moments.

So free your X-Wing from the swamps. Listen to yourself and the world around you. Be amazed by all that is possible.

"That's no moon, it's a space station."

-Obi Wan Kenobi

The Millennium Falcon is chasing a Tie Fighter. It is heading towards a large round object in the sky that Luke incorrectly identifies as a moon. No one seems concerned until that look in Obi Wan's eyes. Because it isn't a moon, it's a space station. Moons are innocuous, ambiguous, general. A space station is specific.

Specificity in improv is the ornate skeleton key which opens the intricately carved door to the Indiana Jones warehouse of toys and possibility. Specificity is where it is at. And yet, it is commonly avoided. Here are the two main reasons why:

1. Fear of closing options
2. Fear of commitment

Fear of Closing Options

It occurs to many of us on stage that if we get too specific we shrink our world. I claim the contrary is true. I believe specificity brings the world we create on stage into vivid Technicolor. The more details we know about our physical surroundings, the history of the characters, the intricacies of the relationships, the creaking the basement door makes, etc, the more possibilities present themselves. And the great thing about those possibilities, which spring from specificity is that they serve the world, the moment, the story at hand.

At the start of any improv game or scene or form, everything is possible. This is daunting because how do we choose; too many possibilities leads to feeling overwhelmed, causing us to shut down. All you need in that moment is one specific detail, and suddenly part of the blank page is colored in, which presents more specific possibilities that exist in that world. And then, instead of everything to choose from, you have relevance to choose from. Specificity does not close doors and shrink worlds. Specificity leads to more specificity, which brings the world in front of you into breathtaking detail.

Fear of Commitment

Then there are those times when we avoid specificity because we fear that once we put it out there we must commit to it. And what if it's wrong, or boring, or not what our partner had in mind, or illogical or boring. By giving into your Judge's Table you make room for the type of judging and censoring that leads to generalizing, negotiating, asking permission and questions. It leads to:

"What is that thing?"

"I don't know, but it is definitely something."

"What should we do?"

"We should probably leave it alone."

It leads to boring improv.

Let me say this again: Your idea is good enough. It is more than good enough. It is the beginning of something that could be transformative. Commit to the idea in your head, heart or gut, and offer it up as a brush stroke on the page. Your specific will make things clearer for your fellow improvisers, the audience and you. It will take you from being lost and unsure, to being excited and playful.

Ok, we've identified and examined our fears, but how do we actually get specific or practice specificity? Here are some thoughts:

- When you make a physical offer, define at least one specific thing about it. A great exercise to practice this is a simple gift giving exercise.
- **Round 1**
  - Pair off
  - One person gives the other person a mimed object. The person giving the object does not have to know what it is or try to indicate what it is. They can give it

shape, or weight, or size to help their partner visualize. BUT THEY DO NOT HAVE TO PRE-DECIDE WHAT IT IS.
- The receiver says "thank you for this _____" and fills in the blank with something specific.
- Do this back a forth a few times.

Round 2
- Pair off
- One person gives the other person a mimed object
- The receiver says "thank you for this_____" and fills in the blank with something specific and adds one detail about the physical object;
    - ie: "Thank you for this jewelry box with the the dragon on top." "Thank you for this baseball signed by Babe Ruth." "Thank you for this bowl full of jelly beans."

Do this back and forth as many times as you want. You can begin to add two specifics, or as many as you want for practice.
It takes some practice to actually see things that aren't there. That is why the person giving the object can give their physical offer some specificity. Once you begin to trust what you see and add specifics, the skill becomes easier and fun.
- When you create an environment on stage add a specific element to that environment. ie: a door. Then mimic the above exercise and give an additional specific to that door; a

creaky door, a red door, a heavy door, a screen door, a door that doesn't close all the way. Any of these specifics could heighten or further any part of the scene.
- When you are identifying, exploring or heightening a relationship, add a specific about that relationship. Here are some ways to do that:
    o Refer to something that happened in the past.
    o Reveal a secret you have learned about the other person.
    o Reveal a secret about yourself.
    o Honestly question or explore the other person's reaction; ie: "You look annoyed." "You smile a lot, that's one of the reasons I've always liked you." "Your words are saying one thing, but your eyebrows are saying something else." etc.

An extra perk of practicing and using specificity is that it gets you out of your head and connected to the people, environment and actions surrounding you; it also helps you to believe in your ideas.

Being specific in improv will grow your game and bust open where you can go, who you can be and what can happen. It changes the fairly innocuous, general offer of the moon, into the complex, dangerous and unpredictable playground of the Death Star.

> "Who is the more foolish, the fool or the fool who follows him?"
>
> *-Obi Wan Kenobi*

Foolishness is often seen as a bad thing, undesirable, unwise. Yet in Shakespeare, the fools are often the wisest. They are acute observers of human nature and context. They are not bound by impulse control. Their bon mots may not always follow a logical path, but their points are always on target and memorable because of their unique illustrative point of view. Foolishness is vital in improv, it is what frees us to play and discover and do the impossible- surprise.

Foolishness comes easy to some; to others it is not a natural state. It must be rediscovered. We have all done foolish things at some point. It is a folly of which we are all capable.

Let me be clear. By foolishness, I do not mean ridiculous goofy behavior for the sheer masturbatory glee of it. I simply mean letting go of logic.

Logic is a glorious thing, but even Spock and Sherlock let go of logic once in awhile. The good thing is, we are all, by nature, order-seeking beings. Our minds instantly contextualize and make sense of all that we see. The moment we see a person, we categorize them: old, young, hipster, housewife, snob, geek, jock, etc. We do this not because we are jerks, but simply because our minds put our universes in order so that we understand how to operate in the world. We don't even have to try, it's like breathing. Logic always finds a way.

So, in improv, since logic always finds a way, we do not have to work so hard to impose it. We just need to welcome it when it arrives. This frees us up to play and embrace the seemingly illogical. To follow that instinct or accept that offer that your cautious grown-up-three-piece-suit-is-this-going-to-be-on-the-test self says doesn't make any sense. Follow it, accept it, run with it. A new order will be discovered, the construct of this unfamiliar universe will become clear.

Can animals talk in this universe? Yep.

Can inanimate objects come to life? Yep.

Can the Keebler Elf be Secretary of State? Yep.

Can I fall in love with someone because I like the loose button on their coat? Yep.

Can I play poker in Heaven? I hope so.

Yes, yes, yes and yes. The key to all of this foolishness? Commit to it and don't be self-serving about it. I am not encouraging being random for random's sake in order to show the world how random and quirky you are. I am encouraging you to take delight in the unexpected impulse whether it is your own or someone else's. Once you trot down that path, commit to it. Do not run back for the safety of supplies and what you know to be familiar. Everything you need you can find in these woods. And once order presents itself, once the running system of this new world is apparent, play in this new playground. You do not have to tear it down in an effort to be extra foolish or random. You've discovered something new, so explore every nook and cranny. When order presents itself do not see it as confining, be fascinated and discover how everything works in this new universe. Become an expert in it.

The way of foolishness can be a dangerous path, however. There are some improvisers, we've all played with them, we've all been them from time to time, who like to be random because they think it makes them look interesting, smart, edgy, memorable. They will derail a scene or a game or a moment to simply say the random thing in order to swing everyone's attention back to them. This is not foolishness it is selfishness dressed in torn jeans and a wry smile. This is ego, pure and simple. This is not the path of a true Jedi.

Logic would have resulted in the Millennium Falcon and all its passengers surrendering completely to the Death Star, becoming prisoner slaves, doing Darth Vader's laundry and Grand Moff Tarkin's taxes. Selfishness would have resulted in Han Solo and Chewie rushing into a fight dragging Luke, R2 and Obi Wan behind while they all get slaughtered Butch Cassidy and the Sundance Kid style while C3PO whines about doom. Foolishness resulted in everyone hiding in the smuggler's hold, until they could disguise themselves as stormtroopers, rescue the princess, disarm the tractor beam, and, well, make movie history.

Foolishness is embracing the impossible idea; it is listening to that voice inside that is saying "that's interesting," or "that's unexpected," and hitching your star to that wagon. Once you do, tell that story with commitment, selflessness and wonder.

> ## "Never tell me the odds."
> ### *-Han Solo*

There are so many reasons I love Han Solo, this is just one of them. With the Empire in hot pursuit, he does not adopt C3PO's practicality or, in fact, any generic common sense. Nope, he heads straight into an asteroid field regardless of the odds of success.

There's this term that many use in business, in education, in sports and yes in improv. It is practical. It is useful. It is both helpful and harmful. The term is "Best Practices."

What is it?

It defines the high level commonly agreed upon how-to's of playing a game, or doing an exercise or building a scene. For example: when dribbling a basketball it is best to dribble low to prevent the other team from stealing. You're welcome.

How is it helpful?

My theory, and let's face it, this whole book is my theory, Best Practices are best used in training and during that first year of improvising in front of an audience. In improv, they provide a scaffolding on which to construct your individual improv skyscraper. They're there to support you as you build and grow annexes and additional floors, and you must be conscious of them when you are looking at the blueprints to figure out what to build next. You must remind yourself to yes and. You must remind yourself that this game is about engaging in the space and that game is about storytelling and narrative structure, and the next scene should have some swinging door edits for variety. When first learning any new material, best practices are great tools to keep you focused, on track and able to consciously improve—to take ownership of how you as an individual improvise. To metaphor again, they make up the skeleton that makes it possible for you to strengthen and develop your muscles.

How is it harmful?

Best Practices, if adhered to like a fanatical religion, will hold you back. They will limit your perception of what is possible and lead you to the dangerous habit of playing it safe. Skeletons are good, but once we learn to crawl and walk and run and fly, we are not acutely conscious of what our skeletons are doing every moment. We just know we want or need to fly at this particular moment in time. Like a pianist
who has no need of scales in the middle of a concerto, or a dancer that does not consider bar exercises in the midst of a leap, an

improviser needs to trust that the scaffolding is there in order to design with abandon and innovation.

Don't get me wrong, you must continue to take care of your skeleton throughout your career. You must take calcium and do exercises to keep it strong. The same is true in improv. You must keep taking classes and reviewing the basics from time to time. Never become so overconfident that you think you are incapable of breaking a bone; the universe has a funny way of keeping us humble that way.

However, many improvisers fall into the misconception that if one follows the Best Practices to the letter every time they will be guaranteed success every time. And, as has been mentioned many times already, there is no guarantee of success. There is no perfect set of directions for improv, or for anything really. Success is not a perfect execution of a game. I have seen many a short-form game or long-form set that was technically proficient and left me feeling unengaged and uninterested. Technique is important, it's essential, I'm a big fan of it, but it is only half the ball game. We do not remember Michael Jordan simply because of his technique, he was a poet on the basketball court. To achieve that level of poetry in any field you must find the balance of technique and inspiration. I do not mean some ephemeral genius, which is only gifted to a few. I define inspiration as the ability to listen and commit to that internal voice that says "This is the way to go right now, this is the thing to do." Sometimes that voice will suggest the most implausible things, like flying into an asteroid field. In that moment, when you are afraid to fail, when the idea seems crazy, when you are unsure of success, switch C3PO off and fly into the asteroid field. The only way to see if you can navigate it is to do it.

> "The More You tighten your grip, the more star systems will slip through your fingers"
>
> *-Princess Leia*

Control…what a myth. We want it because it ensures our future, whether it's a minute from now or ten years from now, we don't like not knowing what comes next. Or maybe it is that we fear we won't be able to handle what comes next, which is completely the opposite of improv. I'm always amazed that the improv world is peopled by so many control freaks. Some of the best improvisers I know are control freaks. But the most inspired improvisers I know revel in and welcome the chaos. Many of us want guarantees though. We want to know we can be funny and we can be loved and that absolutely nothing will go wrong ever. So, we tighten our grip, and secretly plan even if only for a few split seconds before. We try to control the actions of others by:

- Talking a lot
- By saying "yes but"
- Sometimes by physically manipulating them
- Sometimes we literally put our hands over their mouths
- By deserting them or
- Denying them or
- Not trusting them

Once again, not because we are jerks, but because we want to ensure the future, and because we fear the future. We want to make sure everything comes out alright, and even though everyone else is very lovely, we can't really trust them. It is so very hard to truly surrender control and let the moment be what it is, so very very hard. But there is a divine freedom in letting go, in allowing yourself to fall into another's arms, and it is so much less work because everything is new and amazing and you can't help but be fully engaged.

But how do we do that? How indeed? Here are a few suggestions:

If you know you are a control-loving improviser:

- Don't be the first person out in a scene.
- Make it your goal to make everyone else look great: support and heighten.
- Make the scene about the other person- don't try to be fascinating, be fascinated.
- Love every offer everyone else makes.
- Shorten your offers. Force yourself to speak less. People know what you mean, you do not need to spell it out for them.

Those are just five of thousands of possibilities, but it's a place to start. Try one for a while. See if it works. Then try another one. Then come up with one of your own, you know yourself better than I do.

Control is an illusion. The more you try to control something the less control you have. Just ask the parent of a teenager. So dare to let go, really let go. Seriously what's the worst that can happen? So what if Grand Moff Tarkin blows up your planet, in the end his Death Star is toast.

"There are alternatives to fighting."
-*Obi Wan Kenobi*

Oh, Obi Wan, how right you are.

One of the best bits of improv advice I ever got was it's okay to lose the fight. So many improv scenes devolve into a fight, often because people mistake conflict in a story with fighting. Not true. From a structural point of view, conflict is simply the obstacle standing in the hero's way between them and what they want.

Yet, we cling to fights in improv scenes just like we do in life because we don't want to lose. Oh, but losing is so much fun! You are not sacrificing your point of view; you are simply revealing juicy new information that makes the audience perk up after being lulled into the rhythm of your previous argument.

Nobody likes to watch a fight for very long. After a while it just becomes whiny, and, as an audience member, you cease to care. But if you lose the argument, allow yourself to be altered, peel back another layer of what we thought we understood, suddenly you have re-upped our buy-in and we're hooked again. Just like when Obi Wan acquiesced and allowed Darth Vader to win. And we all sat up a little straighter and thought "Whaaaat? Oh this just got interesting."

So lose the fight, don't give up, just dare to find out what lies underneath the fight.

- Reveal new information
- Express an emotional truth
- Be won over by their argument

Losing a fight in an improv scene doesn't mean you're a weak human being, just that you are a strong improviser.

Because remember:

"If you strike me down I shall become more powerful than you can possibly imagine."

> "All his life has he looked away... to the future, to the horizon. Never his mind on where he was. ...Hmm? On what he was doing."
>
> *-Yoda*

Our brains are miraculous. They truly are. The speed at which they operate feels unfathomable. The mind of an improviser likes to get in that racecar and really open her up and see what she can do. Mix that quick mind with the aforementioned desire to control the future and you fall into the classic bear trap of *planning*.

As improvisers we want everything to go well, we want the audience to have a good time, and, even on the tiniest level, we want to be liked. That's a lot of desires to live up to. The temptation to plan ahead or to discover your preferred path and adhere to it with all your might is ever present. And, by focusing on all the things your game or scene could be, you miss all the exquisite surprise and delight of what the moment in front of you actually is.

I'm talking about being present. And friends, that is hard. It demands that you listen fully and completely to all that surrounds you while at the same time listening to your response to it. It asks you to trust your response while at the same time question it to ensure that you are agenda-free save for what the moment dictates. And it needs you to judge what is playing out, not as you the improviser but as you the character in that moment.

This is advanced level calculus. The concept is easily understood, but the skill is forever in a state of acquisition. Here are some things that might help when you find yourself disconnecting and pre-planning.

- Breathe.
- Open your eyes a little wider to see what lies before you.
- Remind yourself that your partners in crime are geniuses and everything they offer is a platter of potential.
- Believe in your response no matter how mundane or random, it appeared for a reason.
- Do not abandon what is in front of you until you have examined and relished in every possible detail and angle, because it is those details that lead to a much more interesting future.

Lastly, and most difficultly, you must cede control. You are not in control, you are a vital contributor and the strength of your response, which lies in its honesty, adds to the creation of a future more interesting, rich and complex than you could ever have imagined on your own

> "Watch your mouth kid or you'll find yourself floating home."
>
> *-Han Solo*

Profanity. I have no problem with profanity...as long as it makes sense in the scene. All too often profanity is used to shock or show how edgy and uninhibited we are. It's also used in desperation when we feel the audience slipping away we throw in a random "mutha fucka" to grab their attention back. Well, we can all be better than that. Swear if it makes sense, if it comes from the reality of the moment. Otherwise, get over yourself, profanity doesn't make you more interesting; investing in your fellow improvisers and trusting the audience does.

"Laugh it up, Fuzzball"

-*Han Solo*

    To laugh or not to laugh? The answer to that question is not always within our control. Here's my take on it:

    Do everything you can to stay in the reality of the moment. Try everything you can not to break on stage. But if it happens, do not deny it or envelop it in shame. An honest moment of enjoyment is joyous for audience and performer alike. Just don't wallow in it, Fuzzball. The audience knows when it is fake or being used as a tactic to get them to see how charming you are. If it happens, let it happen and then use it in the scene or game, let it be a tool to heighten or discover new information. Get on with it, the Empire still needs to be overthrown and the Millennium Falcon isn't going to fix itself.

> **"I don't know who you are or where you came from, but from now on, you do as I tell you."**
> *-Princess Leia*

Ever feel like there's no reason for you to be onstage because your improv partner has got it covered? They've made every offer? They've manipulated or denied your offers to fit their own agenda? Sometimes they even tell you, in scene, not to speak? And, if they're Michael Scott from *The Office*, they sometimes actually kill you off?

At one time or another we have all been or will be in that position. And, face it, sometimes we're the one putting others in that position. It kind of sucks to feel irrelevant. So what do you do?

One school of thought, if there's no reason for you to be on stage, then why are you there? But you don't want to be the a-hole who just walks off because you feel railroaded and your improv ego has been bruised. Instead, you could just take a moment to figure out why you are necessary in this particular story.

The person you are on stage with obviously wants to be in charge, so what is needed to balance the scene?

- Someone who is terrible at being in charge
- Someone who messes everything up
- Someone who desperately admires the person in charge and wants to be just like them
- Someone who has an huge emotional reaction: positive or negative
- Someone who has to leave to go fetch something the person in charge needs
- Someone to enter and actually be higher status than the person in charge

The list could go on forever. No one likes getting railroaded on stage, and it's hard not to take it personally, but the audience shouldn't have to pay for it. Set your personal outrage aside and serve the story being told or the game being played. If you truly feel the only recourse is to leave the stage, do it within the context of the story. Your first priority is to the audience. You can have it out with your fellow improviser after the show, but on stage in front of an audience is no place to teach someone a lesson or fixate on your own personal reaction.

Another school of thought: if you know how someone improvises, you can truly improvise with anyone. People have their styles and quirks, and they are often apparent within seconds of hitting the stage with them. You can sometimes even get an inkling while hanging backstage waiting to go on from how they talk about improv or how they interact with others. I'm not talking about making snap judgments or pigeon-holing, but if you get a sense of how someone plays then your job as an improviser is to figure out how to play with them.

Can it be a challenge?

Yes.

Are you up to the challenge?

Yes.

Whether you approach it with cynicism or a sense of adventure is entirely up to you.

"Great Kid! Don't get cocky."

-Han Solo

What's the difference between confidence and arrogance?

Confidence is belief in yourself; it's trusting your abilities without having to prove them; it's knowing they're there when they're needed.

Arrogance is belief in yourself above all others; it is belief in yourself at the expense of others; it's believing that being the best is the best you can ever accomplish.

The Emperor is arrogant. Luke could have gone that way had it not been for Han's seemingly cavalier advice.

There comes a point in your development as an improviser when the clouds part, and you get it. You find yourself consistently in the zone; all that training and rehearsing has paid off. It often starts with the first laugh you get from an audience. The first affirmation that yes, you are skilled at this and you are funny. And that first laugh is like high-grade cocaine, once you've had it, you can't get enough. It's what makes you show up to every improv jam, and say yes to every cage match, and convinces you to apply to every improv festival. And it feels great for a while.

Until you have that night that doesn't feel quite right. You want to blame yourself, but that can't be right. So you blame her or him for that offer or that denial or that swipe edit. The next time you're on stage, you can't let what happened before happen again, so you take over, under the misguided assumption that you are "saving" the show. You abandon your scene partner(s) for the audience, you choose clever over honest, you anticipate the future rather than staying in the present, and you come off stage feeling worse than before. It was awkward, it didn't feel right, it wasn't fun, you keep blaming everyone else, even the audience.

And then on the drive home, you just feel like crap. You feel like you've never improvised before, like you've forgotten everything, like it might be better for everyone if you just give up now. And you're terrified to get up there again.

You got cocky kid.

And you're in good company. Every improviser does, more than once in the span of their career. And it's not because you're a jerk. It's just that the heady high of improv is a powerful feeling.

You see, when we first improvise, it just seems so impossible, and beyond any level of fun we ever experienced. So when you actually bust through all those introductory classes and 'yes and' drills and Harold rehearsals and work and inspiration and the genius of others comes together and you have that moment when you're not thinking about who-what-where, or finding the game, or heightening, when instinct simply and beautifully guides your every move, it is exhilarating. And you just get greedy for those moments. Because you are human.

And what happens when you get cocky? You make mistakes. You piss people off. You make your individual achievement more important than the miracle of creating something with the other brilliant flawed humans on stage with you. Not because you are a jerk, but because you are human.

So you fall and learn humility. And you step back up on stage, terrified, as if you are treading on unknown territory. What a wonderful place to be. Because now you get to discover all over again, only this time you're not starting from square one, you're on like square seven. You know some stuff, you just need to remember you know it, and toss in some of that humility. And now you feel confident in a deeper way than before. And you're a better improviser because of it.

So like Han says:

"Great kid!"-feel good about blowing up that Tie Fighter, or nailing that moment in the scene

"Don't get cocky"-remember there are three more Tie Fighters out there, there's more work to be done.

And to jump franchises for a moment: "The needs of the many outweigh the needs of the few." So thanks Han & Spock- you come off all arrogant and stuff, but you are the voice of humility in your respective sci-fi allegories.

"But with the blast shield down I can't see, how am I supposed to fight?"
-Luke Skywalker

There is no whining in improv.

Do not blame the audience. Do not blame your fellow improvisers. Do not fault the suggestion. Do not blame the lack of air conditioning. Do not blame the musicians. Do not whine about the blast shield.

The task before you is only impossible if you give up.

Giving up and casting blame is so tempting. When you know it's not clicking, and you're working way too hard and every offer you make is wooden and mechanical and blaaaaah, it's so easy to:

- Blame the audience for being too stupid to get your advanced, subtle, ahead-of-its-time-humor.

- Blame your fellow improvisers for not getting what you meant, or denying your offer or for not being you.
- Blame the suggestion because who can make anything interesting out of that lameness.
- Blame the lights, sound, chipped paint on the stage, your ponytail holder, the sandwich you ate for lunch, anything at all to explain away the horrible that just kept spilling out of you.

If we whine and blame, it means we don't have to change, we don't have to work. At the beginning, we work a lot; we work hard because we want to absorb everything about improv. As we work, we begin to figure out what works for us as individuals, we get confident and secure in what we know we can do. Then it feels less like work and more like play until the show where it doesn't. When it doesn't work, we need to make sense of it, because, as mentioned before, we are order seeking beings. In the process of making sense of it, outward whining and blaming is so much easier than inward exploration, discovery and change.

I'm not saying that every time there is a weird or mediocre show that each moment must be dissected and analyzed and conquered. Sometimes a bad show is just a bad show. Throughout an improviser's life, however, there are phases when everything feels awkward and leaden. Fear not young Jedi, I have learned that these phases signal periods of growth. This is the time to look at what you do from a new angle, take a workshop, watch how another player plays and try some of their approaches. It is a time to, as Yoda says: "unlearn what you have learned."

Luke thinks it's impossible to defend against the training remote with the blast shield down. He can't see, in the traditional sense, until Obi Wan gives him another way to see. The first instinct when something doesn't work the way we expected is to whine and blame. When you feel this happening in your improv try the following:

- Recap what you know so far and what is needed next
- Fall in love with everything your fellow improvisers do and say
- Breathe and focus on one skill; ie: heightening character, discovering & heightening trouble, simply yes-anding, etc.
- Make the scene about your partner and take your focus off of yourself
- Stretch out with your feelings
- Remember that improv is messy, surrender to the chaos and trust that the answers will present themselves if you are patient

I will say it again, there is no whining in improv. Hold yourself accountable, what can you do? Because let's face it folks, sometimes the blast shield is going to be down whether that is the start of the most fun you've ever had is entirely up to you.

> ## "We're doomed."
>
> ### *-C3PO*

I've spoken a lot in this book about fear and how it gets in the way. I do believe it is the biggest hurdle an improviser, and really any human, faces throughout their career. They might get defter at handling it, but that doesn't mean it isn't there. What is it exactly that we fear?

- Fear of ineptitude
- Fear of being uninteresting
- Fear of being un-funny
- Fear of not securing one's place in history
- Fear of not being liked
- Fear of mediocrity
- Fear of not having it all figured out
- Fear of failure
- Fear of failure
- Fear of failure

So, no matter how we name it, it really comes down to Fear of Failure. Well, let me ease your minds: you are going to fail. You are going to fail over and over again. I could regale you with improv-speak about how it's okay to fail and lead you in all sorts of exercises that get us all to understand, on an academic level, that failure is only as powerful as we let it be. And all of that is true, but it's hard to remember when you are face to face with failure.

We've all been there. We know when we've tanked a scene or blown a game. We've winced at the denial that just came out of our mouths so freely. We've sighed in resignation as we consciously give up on stage. And it feels punch-in-the-gut horrible. It makes getting back in the saddle for that next show nauseatingly difficult. It makes stepping on that stage terrifying.

So, we pull way back, we doubt every idea and instinct, we try only that at which we know we can succeed, we keep failure at bay through control and we let fear win. And of course we all know : "Fear is the path to the Dark Side"

I'm not going to tell you to conquer your fear. I'm not going to tell you that fear is your enemy. I'm not going to tell you to push your fear aside and forge ahead. I'm not going to tell you to be fearless. What I will offer is the suggestion to acknowledge your fear and collaborate with it. Fear is present. It has the same potential as any relationship- it can consume and change you if you let it. Or…
It can motivate you

Say 'Hello' to fear. Shake its hand, and ask why it is here. Examine the particular reason for its shadowy presence. Name it (Like saying 'Voldemort', to reference another influential franchise). Basically break it down into smaller parts to assess the *actual* risk involved. 99% of the time that risk is far more nominal than originally imagined.

It gives you permission to be vulnerable

When we are scared we are very vulnerable, and that is not a bad thing. It's another scary thing, but it's not bad. Being vulnerable means that you are completely open. If you are completely open, you are fully receptive. If you are fully receptive, the amount you can gain, even in a moment, is huge. And just as you can receive, your ability to give is also heightened. And giving and receiving is what improv is all about. Fear not the ooey gooey nougaty center that is you; every time you make yourself more vulnerable, you become more delicious.

It is the well where great strength can be found

This is why I will not tell you to be fearless: being brave is not being fearless, it is taking care of what needs to be done in the face of fear. You've acknowledged your fear, you've opened your heart to what it can show you, it is now time to unleash your nougaty center on the world. Collaborating with your fear makes you stronger. And taking that step forward when fear is still hanging around makes the accomplishment of that step a sweeter victory.

It provides perspective

Like I said before, Fear is present, Failure will happen. Each time we recover from either, we learn that we can, in fact, recover. And fear, in general, is less powerful; Darth Vader has become a little less imposing.

So, go ahead and acknowledge that you are doomed C3PO, just do not resign yourself to doom because it's quite possible that escape pod might lead you to best time of your life.

> "The Force is what gives a Jedi his power. It's an energy field created by all living things. It surrounds us and penetrates us. It binds the galaxy together."
>
> *-Obi Wan Kenobi*

The Force is real ladies and gentlemen. Go ahead and poo-poo with your concrete thinking and scientific theories, but I know the Force is real. It is present all the time, but we are not always aware of it or able to actively access it. And then the *moment* happens. It's the moment when you are not working, when you're not wondering what you should do, when your brain is not split between being present and asking itself what the scene or game needs. Everything just seems to be happening in an effortless way, and you are feeling in command but not in control, fluidly creative without trying, you are feeling free and specific without being consciously random and clever, you are in absolute synchronization with the others on stage. Everything is unfolding in front of you showing you the way. Some folks call it being in the zone. But you and I know it is the Force at work and you have become aware of it in that collection of moments. And it is exhilarating and humbling all at once.

You work so hard for so many years to prepare for it. You take classes and read books and go see shows and join all sorts of groups. You have glimpses of it, fleeting and intoxicating; glimpses which become carrots leading you to the next moment. And after all that work, all that necessary and important work, young Jedi, the moment happens when you are ready to let everything go and surrender yourself to absolute trust-not just in your fellow improvisers but in yourself.

For some of us, we fear trusting ourselves because we equate it with arrogance or selfishness. I find this to be especially true of, but not exclusive to, women improvisers. Arrogance can certainly be a pitfall of trust or over-confidence, but it does not go hand in hand with it. Trusting yourself is not arrogant, it is, in fact, a very giving thing to do. It is finally pushing your shit out of the way so that you can generously give of yourself, your ideas, your flaws and your unique oompity-poo which makes you an invaluable asset. It is not believing that you are the best or that you are right, it is simply believing in yourself without agenda, anger or arrogance.

I have noticed that that kind of trust comes and goes. It is difficult to attain, and once attained, tricky to hang onto. It often comes with age and experience and reps. It frequently comes from optimism rather than cynicism. And though it feels fleeting and ephemeral, you can self-help your way to finding it. You might try: Whenever you want to say "I'm sorry," say "I'm sexy" instead. I learned that from a friend who learned that from an Italian performer. I love it, it is freeing and empowering all at once.

- Instead of fixating on the one thing that went wrong in the scene or game or show, celebrate the many things that went well. It doesn't mean you stop trying to grow, but it begins to silence the judges' table in your head.
- When others compliment you, say "Thank you." Instead of listing all the things you did wrong, just say thank you.
- Before every show, warm up by sharing something embarrassing about yourself.
- Read the paper. Watch the news. Get some perspective.
- Breathe and decide to have fun.

This is not a definitive list, but these things can tip the scales in favor of you becoming aware of the Force more often than not. So put the blast shield down, turn off your targeting computer and trust the Force.

"The Force will be with you, always."

-Obi Wan Kenobi

Remember, the Force is real. It will support you, challenge you and lead you to the greatest surprises. It will plateau without care and diligence. It will weaken without risk and failure. It will fade without play and innovation. Its limits have not yet been discovered. Its mastery requires patience, perseverance and perspective. Never take it for granted and never take it too seriously.

Now go forth and save the world Jedis, one improv at a time.

And in the immortal words of Chewbacca in the final tableau of each movie:

"Rrrrrawwwhhhgarrrrr"

Quotations

"An elegant weapon for a more civilized age"
Star Wars:Episode IV-A New Hope. Dir. George Lucas. Story, George Lucas. Screenplay, George Lucas. 20th Century Fox, 1977.

"Punch it Chewie."
Star Wars: Episode V-The Empire Strikes Back. Dir. Irvin Kershner. Story, George Lucas. Screenplay, Leigh Brackett, Lawrence Kasden. 20th Century Fox, 1980.

"A long time ago in a galaxy far far away."
Star Wars:Episode IV-A New Hope. Dir. George Lucas. Story, George Lucas. Screenplay, George Lucas. 20th Century Fox, 1977.

"During the battle, Rebel spies managed to steal secret plans to the Empire's ultimate weapon, the DEATH STAR" and that "Princess Leia races home aboard her starship, custodian of the stolen plans that can save her people and restore freedom to the galaxy"
Star Wars:Episode IV-A New Hope. Dir. George Lucas. Story, George Lucas. Screenplay, George Lucas. 20th Century Fox, 1977.

"Fear is the path to the dark side. Fear leads to anger. Anger leads to hate. Hate leads to suffering."
Star Wars: Episode V-The Empire Strikes Back. Dir. Irvin Kershner. Story, George Lucas. Screenplay, Leigh Brackett, Lawrence Kasden. 20th Century Fox, 1980.

"You know that little droid is going to cause me a lot of trouble."
Star Wars:Episode IV-A New Hope. Dir. George Lucas. Story, George Lucas. Screenplay, George Lucas. 20th Century Fox, 1977.

"Aren't you a little short for a stormtrooper?"
Star Wars:Episode IV-A New Hope. Dir. George Lucas. Story, George Lucas. Screenplay, George Lucas. 20th Century Fox, 1977.

"Stay on target."
Star Wars:Episode IV-A New Hope. Dir. George Lucas. Story, George Lucas. Screenplay, George Lucas. 20th Century Fox, 1977.

"Stretch out with your feelings"
Star Wars:Episode IV-A New Hope. Dir. George Lucas. Story, George Lucas. Screenplay, George Lucas. 20th Century Fox, 1977.

"Into the Garbage chute flyboy."
Star Wars:Episode IV-A New Hope. Dir. George Lucas. Story, George Lucas. Screenplay, George Lucas. 20th Century Fox, 1977.

"You're all clear kid, now let's blow this thing and go home."
Star Wars:Episode IV-A New Hope. Dir. George Lucas. Story, George Lucas. Screenplay, George Lucas. 20th Century Fox, 1977.

"Do or do not, there is no try."
Star Wars: Episode V-The Empire Strikes Back. Dir. Irvin Kershner. Story, George Lucas. Screenplay, Leigh Brackett, Lawrence Kasden. 20th Century Fox, 1980.

"So certain are you. Always with you it cannot be done."
Star Wars: Episode V-The Empire Strikes Back. Dir. Irvin Kershner. Story, George Lucas. Screenplay, Leigh Brackett, Lawrence Kasden. 20th Century Fox, 1980.

"That's no moon, it's a space station."
Star Wars:Episode IV-A New Hope. Dir. George Lucas. Story, George Lucas. Screenplay, George Lucas. 20th Century Fox, 1977.

"Who is the more foolish, the fool or the fool who follows him?"
Star Wars:Episode IV-A New Hope. Dir. George Lucas. Story, George Lucas. Screenplay, George Lucas. 20th Century Fox, 1977.

"Never tell me the odds."

Star Wars: Episode V-The Empire Strikes Back. Dir. Irvin Kershner. Story, George Lucas. Screenplay, Leigh Brackett, Lawrence Kasden. 20th Century Fox, 1980.
"The More You tighten your grip, the more star systems will slip through your fingers"
Star Wars:Episode IV-A New Hope. Dir. George Lucas. Story, George Lucas. Screenplay, George Lucas. 20th Century Fox, 1977.

"There are alternatives to fighting."
Star Wars:Episode IV-A New Hope. Dir. George Lucas. Story, George Lucas. Screenplay, George Lucas. 20th Century Fox, 1977.

"If you strike me down I shall become more powerful than you can possibly imagine."
Star Wars:Episode IV-A New Hope. Dir. George Lucas. Story, George Lucas. Screenplay, George Lucas. 20th Century Fox, 1977.

"All his life has he looked away... to the future, to the horizon. Never his mind on where he was. ...Hmm? On what he was doing."
Star Wars: Episode V-The Empire Strikes Back. Dir. Irvin Kershner. Story, George Lucas. Screenplay, Leigh Brackett, Lawrence Kasden. 20th Century Fox, 1980.

"Watch your mouth kid or you'll find yourself floating home."
Star Wars:Episode IV-A New Hope. Dir. George Lucas. Story, George Lucas. Screenplay, George Lucas. 20th Century Fox, 1977.

"Laugh it up, fuzzball"
Star Wars: Episode V-The Empire Strikes Back. Dir. Irvin Kershner. Story, George Lucas. Screenplay, Leigh Brackett, Lawrence Kasden. 20th Century Fox, 1980.

"I don't know who you are or where you came from, but from now on, you do as I tell you."
Star Wars:Episode IV-A New Hope. Dir. George Lucas. Story, George Lucas. Screenplay, George Lucas. 20th Century Fox, 1977.

"Great Kid! Don't get cocky."
Star Wars:Episode IV-A New Hope. Dir. George Lucas. Story, George Lucas. Screenplay, George Lucas. 20th Century Fox, 1977.

"The needs of the many outweigh the needs of the few."
Star Trek II: The Wrath of Khan. Dir. Nicholas Meyer. Story: Gene Roddenberry, Harve Bennett, Jack B. Sowards. Screenplay: Jack B. Sowards, Nicholas Meyer, Samuel A. Peeples. Paramount Pictures. 1982.

"But with the blast shield down I can't see, how am I supposed to fight?"
Star Wars:Episode IV-A New Hope. Dir. George Lucas. Story, George Lucas. Screenplay, George Lucas. 20th Century Fox, 1977.

"We're doomed."
Star Wars:Episode IV-A New Hope. Dir. George Lucas. Story, George Lucas. Screenplay, George Lucas. 20th Century Fox, 1977.

"The Force is what gives a Jedi his power. It's an energy field created by all living things. It surrounds us and penetrates us. It binds the galaxy together."
Star Wars:Episode IV-A New Hope. Dir. George Lucas. Story, George Lucas. Screenplay, George Lucas. 20th Century Fox, 1977.

"The Force will be with you, always."
Star Wars:Episode IV-A New Hope. Dir. George Lucas. Story, George Lucas. Screenplay, George Lucas. 20th Century Fox, 1977.

www.ingramcontent.com/pod-product-compliance
Lightning Source LLC
Chambersburg PA
CBHW052109070526
44584CB00017B/2406